31 DAYS TO

Satisfied Soul

JOURNAL

A COMPANION TO

Having a Martha Home
the Mary Way

Sarah Mae

with CHRISTIN SLADE

With deep thanks to Christin Slade for working on and writing this journal with me. She is a dear friend, a beautiful writer, and has a satisfied soul in the One who holds her and loves her so very much.

Thank you, Christin.

Contents

"Satisfy us in the morning with your unfailing love, that we may sing for joy and be glad all our days."

PSALM 90:14, NIV

"The Lord is my chosen portion and my cup; you hold my lot."

PSALM 16:5, ESV

Soul Prep: a Satisfied Soul

AS I HAVE READ ABOUT Mary of Bethany, and pondered her interactions with Jesus, it is evident that she found deep satisfaction in His Lordship, friendship, and teaching. The more I studied the Scriptural passages of her, the more I came to realize that her life, as told in Scriptures, is a picture of the beauty of a surrendered relationship with Christ. It is clear to me that Mary had a satisfied soul, that is, a soul that was deeply satisfied in the One who loved her, accepted her, spent time with her, and taught her.

It is her interactions with and response to Jesus on which this journal study is based. We will look at these interactions and responses and learn from them how to find deep satisfaction in our souls with the One who calls us to relationship with Him.

First things first.

Before you begin the 31-day soul journey, I want you to read each of the below passages and write all your observations when it comes to Mary, her interactions with Jesus, and His responses to her. Feel free to take a few days to do this.

Luke 10:38-42 • John 11:1-46 • John 12:1-8

Write your observations below.

_____

_____

_____

_____

_____

_____

_____

_____

My personal observations from the listed passages of Mary, and how we will go forth with this study, lead me to believe that a satisfied soul . . .

- ✓ Gives itself up
- ✓ Is still
- ✓ Sits at His feet
- ✓ Listens
- ✓ Seeks His word
- ✓ Gives up costly things
- ✓ Loves Him regardless of what people think
- ✓ Is defended by Jesus
- ✓ Waits
- ✓ Goes when called
- ✓ Falls at His feet
- ✓ Pours out her heart
- ✓ Moves Him with her tears
- ✓ Sends for Him when needed
- ✓ Is loved

Therefore these are the things that will guide our study. Here's to a satisfied soul!

Sarah Mae

A Satisfied Soul Gives Itself Up

Day 1

Then Jesus said to His disciples, "If anyone wishes to come after Me, he must deny himself, and take up his cross and follow Me.

MATTHEW 16:24

Follow Jesus

① Receive

In order to be a student (disciple) of the Word, we must fully give ourselves up to the One who loves us so dearly: Jesus. Mary gave herself up to Him—trusting Him, learning from Him, and being vulnerable with Him. Trusting requires vulnerability because it's saying, "Here's my life, all of it, and it's yours. Do as you please. I will do my best to follow."

We will never be satisfied and consistently find our soul in unrest if we continue to hold onto our*selves*. Giving ourselves fully to Him is the foundation for everything else. It means trusting Him with *all* of who we are.

② Reflect

What are you holding onto that's keeping you from fully following Jesus? How can you let go of it so you are free to follow Him?

_____

_____

_____

_____

_____

_____

_____

_____

_____

_____

_____

_____

_____

_____

_____

_____

_____

_____

③ Pray

Ask God to help you learn what it means to give yourself up and fully trust Him with YOU.

_____

_____

_____

_____

_____

_____

_____

_____

_____

_____

_____

_____

_____

_____

_____

_____

_____

_____

④ Remember

Denying yourself brings freedom to serve.

Day 2

Take My yoke upon you and learn from Me, for I am gentle and humble in heart, and you will find rest for your soul.

MATTHEW 11:29

Seek Rest for Your Soul

① Receive

Doesn't it offer such a peace to know that learning from Jesus will help us find rest for our souls? Rest is often snuffed out in lieu of daily demands and when we fail to rest physically, we fail to rest spiritually. If we want our souls to be filled, we have to take the time to stop and learn from the One who knows us best. He knows us and what we need. We simply need to go to Him, and learn from Him.

 # Reflect

What wisdom do you need from the Lord right now that you've been trying to figure out on your own?

③ Pray

Ask the Lord for clarity and Holy Spirit power to be receptive to His teachings as you imperfectly, diligently, follow Him by faith.

④ Remember

If any of you lacks wisdom, let him ask of God, who gives to all generously and without reproach, and it will be given to him. JAMES 1:5

A Satisfied Soul is Still

Day 3

Be still, and know that I am God:
I will be exalted among the heathen, I will be exalted in the earth.

PSALM 46:10

Know Him

 ## Receive

Being still is a sign of knowing who we are in light of who God is. Slowing down to fill our souls with His Spirit is crucial for being satisfied in Him and recognizing Him as God. It's a remarkable thing to accept a place of humility before an Awesome God. Getting still before the King and tuning into His love, power, grace, and sovereignty will help us gain a greater understanding of this truth.

② Reflect

When is the last time you sat still and recognized your place in the face of God's place?

_____

_____

_____

_____

_____

_____

_____

_____

_____

_____

_____

_____

_____

_____

_____

_____

_____

_____

③ Pray

Ask God to help you gain an understanding of knowing who He is in a greater capacity than what you know now.

_____

_____

_____

_____

_____

_____

_____

_____

_____

_____

_____

_____

_____

_____

_____

_____

_____

_____

 # Remember

The great God of the universe wants you to be still and know Him.

A Satisfied Soul is Still

Day 4

Wait for the LORD;
Be strong and let your heart take courage;
Yes, wait for the LORD.

Psalm 27:14

Wait for the Lord

❶ Receive

Waiting can be the hardest thing in the world to do at times. Living in such an instantaneous world, it's easy to give up waiting too quickly. Yet, *not* waiting makes way for some stormy seas in the soul, as well as settling for less than God's best. When we rush into something without taking the time to wait patiently on the Lord, the outcome can be detrimental or at the very least, quite undesirable.

② Reflect

What are you struggling to wait for the Lord on today? Take the time and reflect on the times you've waited on the Lord, and times you've rushed ahead. Write these down and what their outcomes were.

③ Pray

Ask Him to help you wait on Him.

④ Remember

Allowing yourself to be fully satisfied in His timing (which takes vulnerable trust) will make the wait more peaceful.

A Satisfied Soul Sits At His Feet

Day 5

*Now we have received, not the spirit of the world,
but the Spirit who is from God,
so that we may know the things freely given to us by God . . .*

1 Corinthians 2:12

Receive His Spirit

➊ Receive

Sitting at the feet of Jesus means arriving ready to receive the Spirit and what He is teaching. It is a peaceful, comforting place; cosied up and leaning in to hear from your Father who loves you. Imagine a child eager to go sit on the floor and listen to what an adult is getting ready to teach—wide-eyed and ready to receive . . . this is how God desires for you to come to Him. Eager. Willing. Searching. Always hungry for more.

② Reflect

He has so much to share with you, loved one. Are you spending time at His feet, letting Him be the authority over you? What is getting in the way of what He is teaching you?

_____

_____

_____

_____

_____

_____

_____

_____

_____

_____

_____

_____

_____

_____

_____

_____

_____

_____

③ Pray

Ask God to give you the things of the Spirit so they are not hidden from you. His Spirit will not only sustain you but carry you!

④ Remember

He doesn't want you to be confused. You won't understand everything, but He will give you insight as He matures you.

A SATISFIED SOUL
SITS AT HIS FEET

Day 6

*Now this I say, he who sows sparingly will also reap sparingly,
and he who sows bountifully will also reap bountifully.*

2 CORINTHIANS 9:6

Sow Bountifully

① Receive

You cannot learn well from the Master if you never take the time to sit with Him. He wants you to come to Him with a willing spirit so He can teach you and show you His loving-kindness. He loves when you give your time to Him with a cheerful spirit, and He can multiply the time (He knows some of us are barely making it as it is). He has so much to give you. Hang in there, sit with Him, and let Him multiply the fruit of your time together.

 # Reflect

When can you set aside the time to meet with Jesus regularly? Consider this carefully and make it a priority in your day. If you miss a day, don't beat yourself up. All is grace. Keep on.

③ Pray

Ask God to help you make the room to meet with Him and *ask* Him to draw you in. He will!

④ Remember

Start small and work your way up to spending more time with Him.

A Satisfied Soul Listens

Day 7

He who has ears, let him hear.

Matthew 13:9

Hear

① Receive

Sometimes we know what God says, but we turn a deaf ear to it because we're afraid or stuck or content. Oh, but everything He says to us is *for* us and *for* our good! He wants us to mature and grow in our relationship with Him, experiencing His love in deeper and more meaningful ways. This usually happens through pain or getting uncomfortable or being willing to move when we've been content to stay put. Tune into His word and trust it; His spirit is alive within the believer and His word will never come up void.

 # Reflect

Are you willing to hear what the Lord has to say to you? Even if it stings? Even if it requires bringing about some change in your life?

③ Pray

Pray God would give you a heart of reception to hear His words and take them as a loving and gentle guidance.

④ Remember

Listening is a discipline often called meditation. Practice sitting with Him after reading His word and attuning your ear to what the Spirit would teach you from it.

A Satisfied Soul Listens

Day 8

My sheep hear My voice, and I know them,
and they follow Me;

JOHN 10:27

Know His Voice

1 Receive

The more we listen for God, the easier it is to discern His voice. Reading His Word regularly is one of the best ways to do this, but also, simply sitting and listening for Him to speak. God can't speak if you're doing all the talking. If you're new to this, it may not be something you recognize right away, but as we continue to practice, we will know His voice.

② Reflect

Have you ever tried simply sitting and listening for God?

❸ Pray

Ask God to speak to you today. Read His word, then wait and listen for Him.

4 Remember

Knowing His voice means knowing His word.

A SATISFIED SOUL LOVES HIS WORD

Day 9

I have rejoiced in the way of Your testimonies,
As much as in all riches.

PSALM 119:14

① Receive

Rejoicing in the word of God, in learning Who He is, is so satisfying to the soul. We learn the intimacy and awesomeness of the God who created us and wove us together so lovingly when we spend time in His Word. Our soul longs to know Him, and when we feast upon His word, we become more gratified in Him.

Reflect

Have you considered investing in a proper, in-depth Bible study? These times can bring so much enlightenment of understanding who God is and how deep His love is for us.

❸ Pray

Ask God to lead you to the place where He wants you in His word and give you understanding as you read and study it.

_____

_____

_____

_____

_____

_____

_____

_____

_____

_____

_____

_____

_____

_____

_____

_____

_____

_____

_____

_____

 # Remember

You're not seeking merely head knowledge; but learning to enjoy being with Him and His word.

A Satisfied Soul Seeks His Word

Day 10

I shall delight in Your statutes;
I shall not forget Your word.

PSALM 119:16

Do Not Forget

❶ Receive

He wants us to remember His word because He knows that tucking it into our soul glorifies Him and will help us in times of temptation, confusion, and unrest. One of the best ways to remember is to write things down. It's easy to forget even some of the most basic truths and promises when every day life is upon us. Try using a journal, music, sticky notes, 3x5 cards, a white board, notebook, mirror—whatever it takes to help us remember His word.

② Reflect

Consider how you remember His word daily. Do you need to take a few minutes to write down His Word? Also remember to delight in His word and statutes!

_____

_____

_____

_____

_____

_____

_____

_____

_____

_____

_____

_____

_____

_____

_____

_____

_____

_____

_____

③ Pray

Ask the Lord to help you remember. He will pour His Spirit over you to help you bring back to memory those things which He taught you!

4 Remember

Write to remember.

A SATISFIED SOUL IS WILLING TO GIVE UP COSTLY THINGS

Day 11

Looking at him, Jesus felt a love for him and said to him,
"One thing you lack: go and sell all you possess and give to the poor,
and you will have treasure in heaven; and come, follow Me."

MARK 10:21

Store Treasure in Heaven

① Receive

Sometimes God asks us to give up those things which distract us from Him. This is not one of the easiest tasks to follow through on, but when we think of His goodness in the face of those *things* there is no comparison. We have the better thing just having Jesus all by Himself. Recognize what real treasure is—it is not of this world.

 # Reflect

Consider the last time you gave up something for the Lord. Something that was truly costly. If you cannot recall a time, is there something God may be asking of you now?

③ Pray

Ask God to clearly reveal what He wants of you for Himself.

4 Remember

Holding on to something is more costly than letting it go for Him.

_____

_____

_____

_____

_____

_____

_____

_____

_____

_____

_____

_____

_____

_____

_____

_____

_____

A Satisfied Soul is Willing to Give Up Costly Things

Day 12

And He said to them, "Follow Me, and I will make you fishers of men. Immediately they left their nets and followed Him."

MATTHEW 4:19-20

Count the Cost

① Receive

When Jesus called the disciples to follow Him, they did so without hesitation. In fact, they dropped what they were doing—they stopped their work right in the middle of it—to follow the call of Jesus. Following His call was way more important than their work.

 **Reflect**

How often is Jesus calling you throughout the day to stop what you're doing and answer His call?

_____

_____

_____

_____

_____

_____

_____

_____

_____

_____

_____

_____

_____

_____

_____

_____

_____

_____

_____

③ Pray

Ask God to help you heed His voice when He's drawing you in—to let go of the work at that moment and meet with Him.

# Remember

Following the call of Jesus will cost you something.

A Satisfied Soul Loves Him Despite What People Think

Day 13

*For whoever is ashamed of Me and My words,
the Son of Man will be ashamed of him when He comes in His glory,
and the glory of the Father and of the holy angels.*

LUKE 9:26

Don't Be Ashamed

 **Receive**

When our soul is satisfied in Christ, it is secure in Christ and there is no room for being ashamed of who we are in Him and what we believe about Him. It's no secret that following the Gospel is counter-cultural to this world. There will be people who come against not what, but Who we believe. Stand firm and remember He is with us and for us; we do not have to walk alone.

 # Reflect

Do you find yourself hesitating when giving God glory where His glory is due in the midst of other people? If you do, sit with this a bit: why? Why the struggle?

③ Pray

Ask God to give you the courage to be open about Him and Truth.

_____

_____

_____

_____

_____

_____

_____

_____

_____

_____

_____

_____

_____

_____

_____

_____

_____

_____

④ Remember

He wants you to trust Him and not be ashamed of Him.

Day 14

For I am not ashamed of the gospel,
for it is the power of God for salvation to everyone who believes,
to the Jew first and also to the Greek.

ROMANS 1:16

Trust the Power of God

① Receive

The gospel, the good news that He has come to redeem His loves if we would turn to Him with all our hearts, has saving power. Salvation comes to those who believe and receive Him, all of Him and all that comes with knowing and following Him. Stand confident in His holy, kind, merciful work. When shame comes in, kick it out! We are redeemed and made righteous because of Jesus, and we have nothing to be ashamed of.

 Reflect

Take time to search the source of the shame or denial you may experience about God. Why might you feel this way?

_____

_____

_____

_____

_____

_____

_____

_____

_____

_____

_____

_____

_____

_____

_____

_____

_____

_____

_____

③ Pray

Ask God to reveal hidden hurts or places of distrust that might be allowing the truth to be shamed in your heart.

④ Remember

The foundation of everything you are in Christ must begin with giving all of yourself to Him.

A Satisfied Soul
Is Defended By Jesus

Day 15

*For the LORD will plead their case
And take the life of those who rob them.*

PROVERBS 22:23

Know He Pleads for You

① Receive

Satan is a thief and He has tried since the beginning of Creation to rob us of all God has for us. But God—God has always defended His people. He defends *us*, you and me because He *delights* in us. When we see ourselves as "less than," He is right there in our spirit to speak truth; we just have to listen to it. We are His and nothing can snatch us from His hand!

 # Reflect

Do you feel like the enemy is beating your door down with lies of defeat? Remember Who your defender is.

_____

_____

_____

_____

_____

_____

_____

_____

_____

_____

_____

_____

_____

_____

_____

_____

_____

_____

③ Pray

If you find yourself tangled in what you're being told and what is true, pray that God would make the truth known to you. Ask for His defense against the enemy.

④ Remember

God has already won the battle!

Day 16

*As for me, You uphold me in my integrity,
And You set me in Your presence forever.*

Psalm 41:12

① Receive

Walking in integrity is so rewarding and God honors His people when they walk in integrity. There are times we will be tempted to step over that line when it seems to be the easier road, but we have power in the Holy Spirit to resist temptation, and we have His loving permission to approach His throne of grace when we are faltering. Our Father will uphold our integrity as we pray for strength, rely on Him, and walk in truth.

 # Reflect

Is there something you're struggling with right now which is putting your integrity on the line? What is it?

_____

_____

_____

_____

_____

_____

_____

_____

_____

_____

_____

_____

_____

_____

_____

_____

_____

_____

③ Pray

Ask God for wisdom in order to overcome the struggle that might be threatening your integrity. Spend time with Him and ask Him to help you trust Him.

④ Remember

He defends His people.

A SATISFIED SOUL
WAITS

Day 17

Our soul waits for the LORD;
He is our help and our shield.

PSALM 33:20

Wait

 **Receive**

Often when we ask the Lord for something, He doesn't answer right away. It could be for healing, having a baby or adoption, missionary or ministry, buying a house, taking a job, or whatever else. God always has a perfect plan even when we may be willing to settle for what we see as our best. But God sees the bigger picture; He has a heavenly perspective, and sometimes that requires a wait. Waiting can be especially difficult when we don't see what He sees, but trust the One who knows the end from the beginning and who works all things out for our good.

② Reflect

Is there something you are waiting on God for? Take this time to focus on praising Him rather than the discomfort of the wait.

③ Pray

Pray the scriptures back to God . . . thank Him for Who He is and tell Him you trust Him with the decision. Praise him in the waiting!

 # Remember

Waiting is actively trusting in God, His character and timing.

A Satisfied Soul Waits

Day 18

*For we through the Spirit, by faith,
are waiting for the hope of righteousness.*

GALATIANS 5:5

Trust in the Hope of Righteousness

① Receive

The battle between flesh (our sinful selves) and spirit (the intertwining of the Holy Spirit with ours) can be an exhausting and frustrating one. We want to be pleasing to God and walk in holiness, but we fail day after day and struggle with the reality that sin dwells in us. But take heart! The battle is already won if we know Him. According to Hebrews 10:14, we are perfect according to heaven because of Jesus. So we walk out our flesh and our maturing on this earth, but Jesus has done it. We are righteous because of Him. Praise God!

 # Reflect

Perfection in our eyes and perfection in the eyes of God are different. Perfection according to our salvation is that we are complete because of Jesus in the eyes of heaven. Take rest and strive no more; He is doing the work in you, completing who we already are. Wild isn't it?

③ Pray

Ask God to show you His perfect will and help you leave yours behind.

④ Remember

Striving for earthly perfection robs us of passion. If you know Him, you can rest in His completed work.

A SATISFIED SOUL GOES WHEN CALLED

Day 19

Fight the good fight of faith; take hold of the eternal life to which you were called, and you made the good confession in the presence of many witnesses.

1 TIMOTHY 6:12

Fight for the Eternal

① Receive

This world and the dark one who is over it, the enemy, will seek to devour you; count on it. But if you know Him, you are sealed with Him and have eternal life, and nothing can take your soul from Him. So fight the good fight of faith. Trust God no matter what, and cling to the hope that is before you. You are His and He loves you. Let your soul take rest; you are secure in His eternal love.

② Reflect

Are you too focused on the things that won't last and neglecting those which are eternal? Consider creating a list of what you work toward in the natural and what you can fight for in the eternal.

 **Pray**

Ask God to open your eyes to see the eternal things so you can fight for them in your own life. This is the life to which you were called.

Remember

The eternal are the only things that will last.

Day 20

Therefore I, the prisoner of the Lord, implore you to walk in a manner worthy of the calling with which you have been called, with all humility and gentleness, with patience, showing tolerance for one another in love.

EPHESIANS 4:1-2

Walk Worthy in Your Calling

① Receive

God has called us into glory with Him. What a beautiful, holy calling to walk with Him in grace and truth. What an honor and responsibility to walk worthy of His name. Let's allow the Spirit to dress us in humility and gentleness and love. You don't have to strive, you just have to obey and trust and rely on His work in you.

 # Reflect

How is your walk with God? Would you say you are walking in a manner that is worthy of Him? What are some areas you need to surrender to Him as He is molding you towards holiness?

③ Pray

Pray to be dressed in the Fruit of the Spirit as you go forth to do what God is calling you to do.

 # Remember

You are called to walk in a manner worthy of your God.

A Satisfied Soul Falls At His Feet

Day 21

Present yourselves to God as those alive from the dead, and your members as instruments of righteousness to God.

Romans 6:13b

Surrender

1 Receive

When we fall at the feet of Jesus, it is a sign of surrender. We are giving our will to Him and offering ourselves up for His purposes. We are allowing Him to use us as an instrument of righteousness. Realize that our strength is not enough and we need Him to carry us through what He's asking of us.

 # Reflect

Do you feel heavy under your own yoke or the yoke of others? Drop it at the feet of Jesus so He can wrap you in lighter garments. What's weighing you down?

_____

_____

_____

_____

_____

_____

_____

_____

_____

_____

_____

_____

_____

_____

_____

_____

③ Pray

Ask God to show you the weight you've been walking under and release it to Him today.

# Remember

The weight of His glory is lighter than the weight of yours.

A Satisfied Soul
Falls At His Feet

Day 22

For all of us have become like one who is unclean, And all our righteous deeds are like a filthy garment; And all of us wither like a leaf, And our iniquities, like the wind, take us away.

ISAIAH 64:6

Empty Yourself

① Receive

Until we come to the Lord empty of everything, we will struggle in our own flesh and deeds. Without Him, everything we do is like a filthy garment because He wants us, not just our deeds. He wants our whole hearts because He loves us so. When we come to Him emptied of everything, He places His robe of righteousness around us and He delights in us. Nothing can be done apart from Christ—otherwise it withers.

 # Reflect

What works are you holding onto that are robbing you of peace and fulfillment in the Lord alone?

_____

_____

_____

_____

_____

_____

_____

_____

_____

_____

_____

_____

_____

_____

_____

_____

_____

➌ Pray

Ask God to help you empty your self, your deeds, your ambitions before Him so He can fill you with His own. Ask Him for understanding of works and His righteousness.

④ Remember

A cup that is already full of something good cannot be filled with His best.

A Satisfied Soul
Pours Out Her Heart

Day 23

Answer me when I call, O God of my righteousness!
You have relieved me in my distress;
Be gracious to me and hear my prayer.

PSALM 4:1

Pour Out Your Distress

① Receive

When we are in distress or struggling with something, we don't need to hold it in trying to make sense of it all. Instead, we pour it out to the Lord. We share with Him every detail of our distress, our pain, our confusion, our frustration, and we allow Him to lead us to the waters of His truth and grace and insight. As we lay all of ourselves and our emotions out to Him, we remember that He cares for us. He desires to give relief to our weary bones.

② Reflect

What is causing struggle or distress in your life that you need to pour out to God and let Him handle? What in your life do you feel trapped by?

❸ Pray

This is an opportunity to pour out all those stresses, worries, and frustrations to Him. He can handle them!

 # Remember

No one can carry your burden the way the Lord can. He is gracious.

A Satisfied Soul Pours Out Her Heart

Day 24

Lord, all my desire is before You;
And my sighing is not hidden from You.

Psalm 38:9

Keep Nothing Hidden

① Receive

We can trust God with the desires and fragility of our heart. He knows them before we bring them to Him, yet He still invites us to bring them to Him. His desire is for us to trust Him with everything: our dreams, hopes, failures, mistakes, and longings. Everything that makes our hearts what they are is not hidden from Him.

 Reflect

What desires are in your heart that you need to pour out to Jesus? Lay them all out.

③ Pray

Pray that He will whittle your desires down to those that are His.

Remember

Fleshly desires will only rob us of His desires.

A Satisfied Soul
Knows Her Tears Move Him

Day 25

A Prayer of the Afflicted when he is faint and pours out his complaint before the LORD. Hear my prayer, O LORD! And let my cry for help come to You.

PSALM 102:1

Cry for Help

① Receive

Did you know crying, really crying, is actually an extremely healthy stress reliever? God created our bodies to physically release certain emotions to relieve stress. It also releases emotional tension. Sometimes we just need to go to God to cry about all the things. When we try so hard to be strong on our own, we are left with a burden that we weren't meant to carry. Tears of repentance and need become tears of redemption and restoration. He sees our tears and they move Him because He cares for us.

 **Reflect**

What have you been holding in, holding back, holding onto that you just need to let out to the Lord?

_____

_____

_____

_____

_____

_____

_____

_____

_____

_____

_____

_____

_____

_____

_____

_____

_____

_____

_____

_____

③ Pray

Don't be afraid to let the tears fall as you talk with God about those burdens on your heart today.

 # Remember

Your tears, your pain, your burdens matter to Jesus.

A Satisfied Soul
Knows Her Tears Move Him

You have taken account of my wanderings;
Put my tears in Your bottle.
Are they not in Your book?

Psalm 56:8

Know He Holds Your Tears in a Bottle

① Receive

Our tears are treasured by the Lord. They are not seen as aggravating, unreasonable, annoying, or unnecessary. God wants to strengthen us in the areas where we feel weak, helpless, or hopeless. Admitting it to Him is half the battle and releasing it through tears is so valuable to Him.

② Reflect

Don't feel like you only need to cry once in a while—do it as often as you need to because He never tires of your need for Him.

_____

_____

_____

_____

_____

_____

_____

_____

_____

_____

_____

_____

_____

_____

_____

_____

_____

_____

③ Pray

As you pray and recognize your need for releasing it all to Him, understand just how valuable you are when you come to Him in prayer. He delights in being with you!

_____

_____

_____

_____

_____

_____

_____

_____

_____

_____

_____

_____

_____

_____

_____

_____

_____

④ Remember

He collects your tears. He knows and accounts for all your days; He sees you, right to the depth of your soul. You are known and loved.

A Satisfied Soul
Sends for Him When in Need

And He has said to me, "My grace is sufficient for you, for power is perfected in weakness." Most gladly, therefore, I will rather boast about my weaknesses, so that the power of Christ may dwell in me.

2 Corinthians 12:9

Trust His Grace is Sufficient

1 Receive

Grace. Do you struggle to receive grace when your need is great? God freely offers us His grace to empower us and strengthen us. God wants our faith to rest on Him, not on our own wisdom or that of other people. We don't need to fill our needs with our own understanding or ideas. We simply seek Him out and receive the grace He offers.

② Reflect

Grace isn't just a feeling, it's an empowerment of Christ in us to keep on. What do you need to release so you are free to serve Jesus without burden?

③ Pray

Release your needs to the Lord . . . hold nothing back. Then, receive what He has for you. Grace. Restoration. And His power to walk in freedom.

4 Remember

Your weakness glorifies Christ.

A Satisfied Soul Sends for Him When in Need

I can do all things through Him who strengthens me.

PHILIPPIANS 4:13

Know He Strengthens You

① Receive

Admitting our need for Christ is an important step to receiving His strength. If we hold on to pride or arrogance, we won't be able to accomplish much in Christ because we'll be working out of our weakness. But with Him, all things are possible. He is our strength.

② Reflect

Are you holding back from calling on the Lord's help? What is holding you back and why?

_____

_____

_____

_____

_____

_____

_____

_____

_____

_____

_____

_____

_____

_____

_____

_____

_____

_____

③ Pray

God will always answer the call of His people—admit to Him you need Him and why.

_____

_____

_____

_____

_____

_____

_____

_____

_____

_____

_____

_____

_____

_____

_____

_____

_____

_____

Remember

He will hold you up.

A Satisfied Soul
Knows it is Loved

In this is love, not that we loved God, but that He loved us and sent His Son to be the propitiation for our sins.

1 John 4:10

Recognize He Loved First

① Receive

We are able to love because Christ loved us first. Isn't that an empowering thought? Think about how we have sinned against a Holy God and how He continues to love us through it anyway. That is a powerful, beautiful, awesome love! And it should spur us on to love Him and love others knowing the depth of our very own need of His love.

 # Reflect

Think about just how much God loves you. Think about what He went through so you weren't separated from Him forever. Consider just how valuable you are to Him!

❸ Pray

Thank God for His love for you today and ask for an even greater understanding of it.

④ Remember

Jesus loves you enough to die for you.

A Satisfied Soul Knows it is Loved

Day 30

See how great a love the Father has bestowed on us, that we would be called children of God; and such we are. For this reason the world does not know us, because it did not know Him.

1 John 3:1

Know You're a Child of God

① Receive

God's love for us is so great that He adopted us as His own children. Think about that! It's important to cling to this truth because when the world comes up against us hard, because it doesn't know Jesus, we need to be able to rest in His love. *His love is enough.* Love from the world is empty. Knowing we are loved by the Almighty God is a sure security.

 # Reflect

What makes you struggle to believe you are loved by God and that you are His?

③ Pray

Lay down those things of the world to which you cling more than to Him. Ask Him to help you know His love for you.

 # Remember

Only the love of Christ will satisfy.

Day 31

What Has the Lord Taught You?

① Receive

A satisfied soul is at rest in the One who gives identity, security, and love. As you sit at the feet of Jesus, learning from Him, being still before Him, offering all of yourself to Him, He will meet your deepest needs and satisfy your thirsty soul. *You are so loved.*

 **② Reflect**

You have spent a month digging into the word and your soul and pondering the deep things of Christ. What has the Lord taught you? What has He most impressed on you during this time that you want to remember?

③ Pray

Take today to thank Him for all He has done over the past month. Ask Him what's next.

④ Remember

Your soul can only be fully satisfied in Him alone.

Look for Signs You Need to Rest

(Taken from "Intimacy with God: Listening to God" Navigator Discipleship Tools)

Am I tired and weary?

MATTHEW 11:28-30

Am I hungry and thirsty?

Am I confused? Do I need direction?

Am I dissatisfied?

PSALM 62:1

Am I longing for more?

PSALM 42:1

LOOK FOR SIGNS YOU NEED TO REST **137**

Am I in need of renewed strength?

ISAIAH 41:1

"Satisfy us in the morning with your unfailing love, that we may sing for joy and be glad all our days."

Psalm 90:14, NIV

"The Lord is my chosen portion and my cup; you hold my lot."

Psalm 16:5, ESV

Sarah Mae has a past that would be her present if it weren't for Jesus. His wild saving grace and gentle leading keep her in awe. She is the coauthor of *Desperate: Hope for the Mom Who Needs to Breathe*, and author of the books, *Having a Martha Home the Mary Way: 31 Days to a Clean House and a Satisfied Soul* and *Longing for Paris: One Woman's Search for Beauty, Adventure, and Joy . . .Right Where She Is.*

Sarah and her family make their home in the beautiful Amish countryside of Pennsylvania where she often ponders what life would be like if she actually *finished* all the laundry. You can find her writing at **SarahMae.com.**

Twitter.com/SarahMae
Facebook.com/sarahmaewrites
Instagram.com/sarahmaewrites

Christin Slade is a Type-A, details-oriented, driven writer, virtual assistant, ghost-editor, and author. She loves working with others to help them make their vision come to fruition, and she thrives under pressure. Christin is a child of God, a wife to a very supportive and loving husband, and homeschooling mother of seven. She is learning daily what it means to live and love by grace. You can find her at **ChristinSlade.com.**

Twitter.com/ChristinSlade
Facebook.com/ChristinWrites
Instagram.com/ChristinSlade

Sarah Mae's Books

Having a Martha Home the Mary Way: 31 Days to a Clean Home and a Satisfied Soul

Desperate: Hope for the Mom Who Needs to Breathe (with Sally Clarkson)

Longing for Paris: One Woman's Search for Joy, Beauty, and Adventure . . .Right Where She Is

Made in the USA
Middletown, DE
04 April 2016